Discover the 1930s

A learning resource guide by Janelle Diller

DISCOVER THE 1930s

By Janelle Diller

Copyright 2019 by Janelle Diller. All rights reserved. Published in the United States by WorldTrek Publishing, 121 East Vermijo, Colorado Springs, CO 80903
The content is this guide is intended for classroom use and may be copied and reproduced for that purpose only. All other uses must be approved of in writing by the author prior to use.
ISBN 978-1-936376-67-4

Never Enough Flamingos ♦ *Never Enough Sisters* ♦ *Never Enough Lilacs*
www.janellediller.com

Parents, Teachers, and Learners,

I've designed this learning to give you a greater understanding of the 1930s in the United States. I created these activities with the *Never Enough* series in mind; however, most of the activities work very well independently of the book. If you're using other books from that era such as *Grapes of Wrath* or *Of Mice and Men*, you'll find plenty of activities that easily compliment your content.

Social studies and, more specifically, history were always my favorite subjects in school, even when I was unfortunate enough to have a teacher who didn't love it as much as I did. In college, I chose history as my major and was blessed with professors who were passionate about the subject. They introduced me to using primary sources for my own research, which only cemented my love for the discipline. I remember the excitement of pouring over newspapers from the 1830s and '40s for my senior research project and coming away with so much more than just the information I needed for my topic. I lived and breathed that era long after my paper was done. Today, the internet has provided as with opportunities to discover even more information that I could have only dreamed about having access to as a student decades ago.

My hope is that learners will discover this as well and along the way pick up valuable critical thinking skills as they dig deeper into the decade.

Of all the activities I've included, the most difficult ones to design were the ones focused on sexual abuse and its ripple effects. In some communities and schools, the activities can all be used and will be valued as they are. In others, it's much more difficult to have any kind of conversation about sexual abuse. At the very least, I hope educators can provide the "Resources to Tap" page for students who have been affected by sexual abuse.

And finally, this is a work in progress. I'm especially grateful for the insights from Amber Neighbor, ELA/FLA teacher in the Buhler, Kansas, school system. Her fresh perspective added depth and breadth to many of these activities. I hope as you use this learning resource and come up with new ideas to make the activities more effective in your classroom that you'll share your ideas with me at janelle@janellediller.com. In turn, I'll update the guide for future users and will share the changes with other current users. We're all in this together.
~Janelle Diller

Learning Standards

Learning Standards

The activities in this learning resource address many Common Core standards, particularly in English language arts, history/social studies, and writing. Some of the activities also lend themselves to creatively extend the learning about the 1930s in science, math, and art. The standards listed below are for grades 11 and 12, but the activities can also be used for younger grades.

Literacy
- CCSS.ELA-LITERACY.RL.11-12.1: Cite strong and thorough textual evidence to support analysis of what the text says explicitly as well as inferences drawn from the text, including determining where the text leaves matters uncertain.
- CCSS.ELA-LITERACY.RL.11-12.1: Determine two or more themes or central ideas of a text and analyze their development over the course of the text.
- CCSS.ELA-LITERACY.RL.11-12.3: Analyze the impact of the author's choices regarding how to develop and relate elements of a story or drama.
- CCSS.ELA-LITERACY.RH.11-12.1: Cite specific textual evidence to support analysis of primary and secondary sources, connecting insights gained from specific details to an understanding of the text as a whole.
- CCSS.ELA-LITERACY.RH.11-12.2: Determine the central ideas or information of a primary or secondary source; provide an accurate summary that makes clear the relationships among the key details and ideas.
- CCSS.ELA-LITERACY.RH.11-12.6: Evaluate authors' differing points of view on the same historical event or issue by assessing the authors' claims, reasoning, and evidence.
- CCSS.ELA-LITERACY.RH.11-12.7: Integrate and evaluate multiple sources of information presented in diverse formats and media in order to address a question or solve a problem.
- CCSS.ELA-LITERACY.RH.11-12.8: Evaluate an author's premises, claims, and evidence by corroborating or challenging them with other information.
- CCSS.ELA-LITERACY.RH.11-12.9: Integrate information from diverse sources, both primary and secondary, into a coherent understanding of an idea or event, noting discrepancies among sources.
- CCSS.ELA-LITERACY.WHST.11-12.2: Write informative/explanatory texts, including the narration of historical events, scientific procedures/experiments, or technical processes.
- CCSS.ELA-LITERACY.WHST.11-12.4: Produce clear and coherent writing in which the development, organization, and style are appropriate to task, purpose, and audience.

Learning Standards (con't)

- CCSS.ELA-LITERACY.WHST.11-12.5: Develop and strengthen writing as needed by planning, revising, editing, rewriting, or trying a new approach, focusing on addressing what is most significant for a specific purpose an audience.
- CCSS.ELA-LITERACY.WHST.11-12.6: Use technology, including the Internet, to produce, publish, and update individual or shared writing products in response to ongoing feedback, including new arguments or information.
- CCSS.ELA-LITERACY.WHST.11-12-7: Conduct short as well as more sustained research projects to answer a question or solve a problem; narrow or broaden the inquiry when appropriate; synthesize multiple sources on the subject, demonstrating understanding of the subject under investigation.
- CCSS.ELA-LITERACY.WHST.11-12.8: Gather relevant information from multiple authoritative print and digital sources using advanced searches effectively; assess the strengths and limitations of each source in terms of the specific task, purpose, and audience; integrate information in the text selectively to maintain the flow of ideas, avoiding plagiarism and overreliance on any one source and following a standard format for citation.
- CCSS.ELA-LITERACY.WHST.11-12.9: Draw evidence from information texts to support analysis, reflection, and research.
- CCSS.ELA-LITERACY.WHST.11-12.10: Write routinely over extended time frames and shorter time frames for a range of discipline-specific tasks, purposes, and audiences.
- CCSS.ELA-LITERACY.SL.11-12.1: Initiate and participate effectively in a range of collaborative discussions (one-on-one, in groups, and teacher-led) with diverse partners on grades 11-12 topics, texts, and issues, building on others' ideas and expressing their own clearly and persuasively.
- CCSS.ELA-LITERACY.SL.11-12.2: Integrate multiple sources of information presented in diverse formats and media (e.g., visually, quantitatively, orally) in order to make informed decisions and solve problems, evaluating the credibility and accuracy of each source and noting any discrepancies among the data.
- CCSS.ELA-LITERACY.SL.11-12.4: Present information, findings, and supporting evidence, conveying a clear and distinct perspective, such that listeners can follow the line of reasoning, alternative or opposing perspectives are addressed, and the organization, development, substance, and style are appropriate to purpose, audience, and a range of formal and informal tasks.
- CCSS.ELA-LITERACY.SL.11-12.5: Make strategic use of digital media (e.g., textual, graphical, audio, visual, and interactive elements) in presentations to enhance understanding of findings, reasoning, and evidence and to add interest.

Research Resource

The Federal Writers' Project

The Federal Writers' Project, 1936-1940, was a US federal government project to employ white collar workers, such as historians, writers, teachers, and librarians, who had lost their jobs as a result of the Great Depression.

It's an amazing treasure trove of first-person accounts of Americans who lived at the turn of the century. Among the thousands of documents, you'll find first-hand reports of being a slave, meeting Billy the Kid, surviving the 1871 Chicago fire, or being a pioneer. You'll find an interesting collection of photos, as well. In fact, all of the photos in the guide are from the Federal Writers' Project. The best part is that they're copyright free, so they can be used for whatever you need.

Whether you're researching the art or music of an era, a vocation such as farming or banking, a location, or a famous person, you'll find the collection to be a rich source of people's experiences. Use this link to read more about your topic: https://www.loc.gov/collections/federal-writers-project/

The Federal Art Project

The Federal Art Project was similar to the Federal Writers' Project. It employed painters, sculptors, muralists, and graphic artists. Other federally funded project for artists included the Public Works of Art Project (PWAP) (1933-34), the Department of the Treasury's Section of Painting and Sculpture (1934-42; renamed the Section of Fine Arts in 1938), and its Treasury Relief Art Project (TRAP) (1935-38).

Use this link to search for what you're researching. As with the Federal Writers Project, you can search by topic, year, location, artist, etc.: https://www.loc.gov/pictures/.

Primary Source Research

For historians, there's nothing better than to find **primary source** information on a topic. This is an artifact, document, diary, photo, autobiography, recording, or any other source of information that was created at the time or event being studied. A book written about the topic is not a primary source even though it may include primary, or original, source information and be very helpful to read. Of course, if the author is someone who was part of the historical event, it may fit into the original source category because the author was present.

Choose an event in history to research.

The event should be something that happened before you were born. For instance, you may want to research an event such as the bank holiday, the passage of social security, the bombing of Pearl Harbor, the bombing of Hiroshima, the passage of the civil rights bill, President Kennedy's assassination, or the moon landing. To get ideas for a topic about the 1930s, spend some time exploring the Federal Writers' Project https://www.loc.gov/collections/federal-writers-project/ or the Federal Art Project https://www.loc.gov/pictures/. By starting here, you'll know whether or not you'll have a enough primary sources for your research.

Before you start to research, here are a few things to consider.

- What do you already know about this event? (It's okay not to know very much about it before hand. Curiosity is your best research tool!)
- Where have you gotten most of your information?
- What does your history textbook say about it?
- What do you expect to discover?

What sources can you find?

Newspapers:
Newspapers from the era are a great resource because editors and reporters are choosing what is important to them or to the readers. Even better, if you have access to multiple newspapers from the era, you'll get more perspectives. Your town's local paper from that era, a newspaper from a larger city in your state, or a newspaper from a large city in another part of the country are all original sources.

- What makes the headlines?
- How do the headlines differ between small town and city newspapers?
- If a city has multiple newspapers that represent different political perspectives, how do they differ?
- What is the primary focus of the articles?
- If you lived at that time and didn't have the advantage of knowing what we know now, what would you think is happening?

Primary Source Research (cont'd)

What resources can you find? (continued)
- If you had been a reporter who wrote about this event, what would have been your prediction about what this event would mean a year from the time of the event?
- What did you learn about the event that you didn't already know?

People:
Another valuable primary source is people who were alive at the time of the event and old enough to remember it. If you're fortunate enough to have a living family member or neighbor who can remember the event, interview him or her. If you don't know of anyone, a local nursing home is likely to have someone old enough to remember. Interview this person. Keep in mind that oral histories are not necessarily accurate reflections of events, but they're very interesting nevertheless because they tell us how people perceived and were impacted by events. Remember, not every question will give you an interesting or important answer (and not every question below fits the research of an event). That's why it's important to ask a lot of questions!

Here are some questions to get you started.
- How old were you when this event happened?
- Describe the moment you heard about this event.
- What was the reaction of the people around you?
- What do you remember about this event?
- Did you or your family see it coming, or were you surprised? Why?
- What stands out in your mind about the event?
- What impact did this event have on you or your family?
- What choices did your family make as a result?
- What choices did you personally make as a result of living through this event?
- How did you get most of your news?
- What was your perception of the President and his role in this event?
- How responsible was he?
- What could he have done to change the course of history?

Never Enough Flamingos ♦ *Never Enough Sisters* ♦ *Never Enough Lilacs*
www.janellediller.com

Primary Source Research (cont'd)

Letters or diaries:
Decades ago, before the age of computers, people wrote letters and kept diaries. The receiver of the letters often kept them. If you know someone who was alive during the time when the event happened, ask if he or she has access to letters from this period and if you can read them. Remember that letters and diaries only reflect how the person experienced the event. They may not be an accurate account of the event itself. Yet they can be a valuable source because it helps us understand what it was like to live during the event.

Here are some things to think about as you read the letters or diaries.
- Does the person write about the event?
- If not, what other things does the person write about?
- Why do you think the person wrote about the event or didn't write about it?
- If the person wrote about it, how does he or she describe the event?
- How is this consistent with or different from the public understanding of the event?
- What else did this person write about that gives you a clearer understanding of the era?

Additional resource:
Remember to use the Federal Writers' Project and the Federal Art Project. Don't give up if your early searches yield nothing. Sometimes you just need to look at the event from a different perspective.

More to think about:
- If you were a student in the 1930s and wanted to research what had happened 80-90 years earlier, what resources would you have had?
- How would you have done the research?
- How does that impact what we think about the era?
- Eighty to ninty years from now, how do you think research will be done?
- What will people understand about our era based on the information that's available?

Primary Source Research (cont'd)

Pull it all together.
Now that you've done your research, pull it all together in a report. Start by organizing it:
- What's your overall understanding of the event?
- If you had to explain the event and the historical significance of it in one minute or less, what would you say? (Start with this idea.)
- How will you tell the story of the event? Chronologically? By perspective? By contradictory evidence? Looking back? By key players?
- What are the major points you have to support your idea? A short paper should have no more than three points. A longer paper can have more. Be careful that you don't have so many points that you confuse your reader or make it difficult for the reader to understand what's most important.
- What are the supporting pieces of information you have for each of your major points?
- What is the conclusion you want your readers to walk away with?

What else will be important to share with your readers?
- What sources did you use that were valuable?
- In what ways were they consistent?
- In what ways did they contradict each other?
- What is important about the contradictions?
- How do you weigh what's accurate?
- How will you incorporate how people experienced the event, which may contradict the public's understanding of the event?
- How can you use how people experienced the event, which supports the public's understanding of the event?
- Be sure to document your sources and identify when you've quoted someone from an interview.

Last, but not least, create.
Create a video blog and talk about the following:
- What did you learn from this exercise about research?
- What did you learn about the reliability of sources?
- What did you learn about the ease or difficulty of accurate research?
- What did you learn about the event itself that you will want to remember?

Pair up with another student and watch each other's video blog. Share your observations:
- What challenges did you have in common? What did you both find easy?
- What did you learn from the other video blog?

Capture History Now

The idea for *Never Enough Flamingos* came when I was in college and had an assignment of interviewing my parents and grandparents for an oral history of our family. I remember sitting with my maternal grandfather—the only grandparent still alive—and asking him questions about the dust bowl and the Great Depression. He told a story of discovering that all of their small herd of cows had gotten into loco weed and died. As he told the story, he began to cry, and in his tears, I could hear him say, "I didn't know how I was going to provide for my family." The event happened more than forty years earlier, and yet the memory of it still evoked strong emotion in him. I knew in my heart that someday I would write a story that captured that moment. My grandfather's story ended up being chapter two of the *Never Enough Flamingos* and one of the important plot points that launched the rest of the story.

Create your own primary source history.

The Federal Writers' Project people had to capture the interview with paper and pencil, transcribe it using a typewriter, and then snail mail their work to the repository. Technology has made it much easier to document these days.

1. Using your phone or video camera, interview someone who is at least 40 years older than you. Do a five-minute interview of this person talking about a historical event he or she experienced.

Here are some interview questions to get you started, but don't limit yourself to these. The <u>most important</u> thing a historian can be is curious:
- What were significant historical moments that you remember?
- What impact did they have on you?
- What choices did you make as a result?
- What was/were the major war(s) during your lifetime?
- How did those wars impact you?
- Who is/was your favorite president? Why?
- How did the president impact the direction of the country?
- Who is/was your least favorite president? Why?
- How did the president impact the direction of the country?
- What was important to you when you were my age?
- What choices did you make as a result?
- What was the most significant technological changes in your lifetime?
- What are the books you remember reading as a teenager? How did those books influence you?
- How did you get national news when you were growing up?
- How is it different today?
- What were the stories on the nightly news or in the newspapers?

Capture History Now (con't)

- Tell about a happy or funny time when you were my age.
- Tell about a sad or disappointing time when you were my age.
- What's a significant memory you have from when you were my age or younger?
- How did that impact you?
- Who is a famous person you remember from when you were a teenager? What did this person do that makes you remember him or her?
- If you could go back to any age or era, what would it be? Why?

1. Now interview a friend around your age. Ask the same questions.

2. Make a video of yourself as you answer the same questions.

What insights/observations do you have about the three interviews?

Capture History Now (con't)

Use the interviews and do one of the following:

1. Take one of the stories you were told and turn it into a short story.
Here are tips to help you write the story:
- Will this be written in first person? Omniscient third person? Omniscient limited?
- Will the story be accurate, or will you fictionalize it?
- Will this be a comedy (everything turns out happy in the end)? Or a drama (it has an unhappy ending)?
- Which person will be the main character?
- Free write for five minutes just describing the character. What you write might not make it into the story, but you'll know more about what the character thinks and feels and how he or she will react to the events in the story.
- Who are the characters in the story?
- Free write for five minutes about them, too.
- Where does the story take place? What description do you need so the reader can see, hear, smell, touch, and feel the location?
- Again, free write for five minutes.
- When does the story take place? What's important about this?
- One more time, free write.
- Identify the major plot points.
- Where is there the greatest tension in the story?
- How does the story end?
- What do you want the reader to walk away with?

2. Write a newspaper account of what you learned.
Remember to start with who, what, where, and when in the first paragraph. Be sure to include quotes from the interview.

3. Create a news station video interview.
Use all three interviews and put them together in editing. Then add music and transitions as well as credits at the end for the people interviewed and the songs used.

Last, but not least, write.
Write one more page. Include the following:
- What did you learn about the person or about an event?
- How did your perceptions of this person or event change as a result of the interview?
- What do wish you would have known about this person or event earlier?

Compare and Contrast

After you've interviewed someone at least forty years older than you, imagine that fifty years from now, your grandchild interviews you. How will you answer these questions? Remember, this is well into the future, so you'll need to do some predicting about what might be answers to these questions fifty years from now.

Here are some questions to answer:
- Who was president when you were a teenager? What do you remember about the presidency?
- What were significant historical moments that you remember from your life up until you graduated from high school?
- What impact did they have on you?
- What choices did you make as a result?
- What was/were the major war(s) during your life up until you graduated from high school?
- How did those wars impact you?
- What was life like for you as a teenager?
- How was your life different at 15 compared to your parents' lives? Your grandparents? Your children? Your grandchildren?
- What was important to you as a teenager?
- What choices did you make as a result?
- What was the most significant technological changes in your lifetime up until you graduated from high school?
- What are the books you remember reading as a teenager? How did those books influence you?
- What were the stories on the nightly news or in the newspapers?
- Tell about a happy or funny time when you were a teenager.
- Tell about a sad or disappointing time when you were a teenager.
- What's a significant memory you have from when you were a teenager or younger?
- How did that impact you?
- Who is a famous person you remember from when you were a teenager? What did this person do that makes you remember him or her?
- If you could go back in time to when you were a teenager, what would you do differently? What advice would you give yourself?

Create a time capsule.
Find things that symbolize the answers to the above questions. In addition, write a letter or create a video blog to be placed in the capsule that explains the answers. To make it extra fun, save the time capsule and open it at a future class reunion 10, 20, or even 50 years from now.

Analyze the News

In the 1930s, people had two primary ways of getting their news: from newspapers and from the radio. Often, cities of any size would have multiple newspapers and would put out morning and evening editions of their papers, as well as special editions if something major happened.

Using newspapers from that era, skim the headlines from the previous year.
* If you would have been a reporter during this time, what would your predictions be about the coming event?
* Choose one of the more prominent topics and read five articles about the topic.
* What do you learn from the articles?
* If you'd lived during that time, what would be your perspective of the world?
* How were the views similar or different from how we view that era today?
* How are newspapers different today than they were then?

Create a newspaper.

After studying the newspapers from the 1930s, create your own first page of a newspaper. Use the Federal Writers' Project for ideas or photos. It's all copyright free, so you can use any of it without violating copyright laws.
* What kind of articles will you include?
* What kind of headlines will you create for your articles?
* How will the writing style differ from newspapers today?

Analyze Today's News

Today, newspapers have a difficult time financially because there are so many competing ways to find information, and so we've lost much of the print media that Americans used to depend on for their news. In 1981, there were 1,730 daily newspapers. By 2016, that number had dropped to 1,286. This is bound to decline even more rapidly of the coming years. Today, 74% of newspaper readers are 45 years or older, even though this group is less the 40% of the population. In contrast, only six percent of 18- to 24-year olds read a newspaper, even though they represent ten percent of the population. An added challenge is that local ownership of papers has dropped significantly. Twenty-five companies own nearly one-third of U.S. newspapers and two-thirds of dailies.

Discuss.
- Why do you think the number of daily newspapers has declined so rapidly?
- Why are newspapers more of a source for news for older readers than younger readers?
- What is the long term impact of this?
- What is the impact of fewer newspapers?
- What is the impact of so few companies owning such a large proportion of newspapers?

In many ways, cable news and major news stations, such as ABC, CBS, and NBC, have replaced the daily newspaper. Just as newspapers of the 1930s had biases, news outlets do too. The internet has also filled much of the void, which brings its own risk since anyone can post anything, true or not. It makes it much harder to sort through what's accurate because the sources are so varied.

Study the news.
Choose a current event that is getting a lot of attention this week. Go to the websites of these news outlets and newspapers:
- ABC
- CBS
- NBC
- CNN
- Fox News
- PBS
- New York Times
- Wall Street Journal
- Washington Post
- Huffington Post
- Brietbart News
- Daily Kos

Analyze Today's News (con't)

Answer these questions on your own.
- What are the top three stories being reported by each site?
- What is the perspective of the news organization?
- What are the similarities in the stories?
- What are the differences?
- What biases do you observe?
- How accurate are these sites in fact checking?
- Which is more important for a news consumer? Bias or fact checking accuracy? Why?
- What insights do you have about news organizations in the United States?

Be a critical thinker.
Here's a site that rates news and research organizations based on their biases: https://mediabiasfactcheck.com. How does this site rate each of the above for their news bias and accuracy? Be sure to click on "[...]" to get a full report.
- How does this change your perspective on the topic you've read about on each site?
- What impact does this have on the news sources you'll choose going forward?

Discuss in small groups.
As a small group, be prepared to share one idea from your discussion with the larger group. Once an idea has been shared, other groups cannot share the same concept. Be ready to have a robust perspective and lots of ideas!

Write.
- What have you learned about news sources?
- What will be important for you as you read newspapers, listen to the news, and surf the internet for news?

Farming

In the 1930s, most farms were small family run endeavors. Often, the land was handed down or purchased by the succeeding generation. Today, most farms are much larger and are corporations.

Here are some sources to explore:
This link is a timeline that describes changes in farm life over the decades.
https://www.agclassroom.org/gan/timeline/1930.htm

These links have additional information about farming over the decades.
http://www.livinghistoryfarm.org/index.html
http://www.ushistory.org/us/49c.asp

Remember that one source you can use to research this is the Federal Writer's Project. There are numerous sources in the project about farming and farm life in the collection.

Compare and Contrast farming today with farming in the 1930s.
- What size farms did people have compared to today?
- What kind of equipment did they have compared to today?
- What were their costs compared to the cot of farming today (make sure you translate into current dollars)?
- What was their income like compared to today (make sure you translate into current dollars)?
- What roles/jobs did farm family members have compared to today?
- Why did people farm then? Today?

Explore:
- Compare and contrast the impact on society as farm culture has changed.
- What was gained and what was lost by having farms family owned?
- Today, what's gained and what's lost by corporations owning and running farms?
- What has been the ripple effect of family farms moving to corporate farms on rural towns, schools, and other family owned businesses?
- Looking into the future, what do you project that it will be like to live in rural America in 20 years?

Making It All Add Up

Add it all up.
Farming has changed dramatically over the decades. Research farming from the 1930s. Here are some sites to get you started. Don't forget to explore the Federal Writers' Project for first-hand accounts of what it was like to farm during the Great Depression.
- Data related to land area of the United States, number of farms and farm acreage, uses of land, land available for crops, land used for crops, and value of farms from various years from 1840 to 2002
- http://agcensus.mannlib.cornell.edu/AgCensus/homepage.do
- For wheat prices: http://www.u-s-history.com/pages/h1532.html
- One family's account from 1928 and 1932: http://www.livinghistoryfarm.org/farminginthe30s/money_23.html

Choose a specific year and a specific location (a county, state, or region).
You might not be able to find specific data for all of the questions below, so based on what you can find, make an educated guess. Make sure you explain the year you've researched and how you came to this educated guess.
- What was the average wheat yield per acre?
- What did an acre of land sell for?
- What did a bushel of wheat sell for?
- What did fuel cost?
- How much fuel did it cost to run a tractor?
- What did a tractor cost?
- Plot out the family finances for a farm.

Do an analysis.
How much money did a farm family make in the 1930s?

Now Compare.
What would the answers be for the above questions for this decade? Don't forget to calculate 1935 dollars compared to today's dollar. Here's a site to help you do this:
http://www.saving.org/inflation/inflation.php?amount=1&year=1935 In other words, just because a bushel of wheat sells for five times as much as it did in the 1930s doesn't mean that a farm makes five times as much.

Present.
Present your findings in a pictorial way. Use graphs, pie charts, pictures from then and now. Use a tool like Piktochart to display your findings to the class.

The Reality of Immigration

Many of the ethnic and cultural or religious groups in the United States immigrated here in waves. For example, Germans, Poles, Irish, Chinese, Vietnamese, Sudanese, and Mexicans have periods where immigration spiked. Don't forget that most African Americans in America trace their roots back to the slave trade. They were certainly immigrants, although not by choice! Some religious groups, such as Jews and Mennonites, also have spikes of immigration. Cat's father's family arrived from the Crimea in the 1880s.

Explore.
Choose a group that immigrated to the United States en masse over a period of several decades. If you know your own ethnic or religious heritage, explore it. If you're not sure, here are some other options that will give you a high level view of immigration up until 1965.
http://libertyellisfoundation.org/immigration-timeline Remember to search the Federal Writers' Project to see if there are any interviews about the group you've selected.

Here are some questions to get you started:
- Who were they?
- Where did they come from?
- Why did they immigrate at that point?
- What is their community like today?
- What did they contribute when they emigrated?
- What did they experience as immigrants?
- What did they have to go through to leave their own country?
- What did they experience as they traveled?
- How were they received in the United States?
- What was the impact on the United States to have so many people of this group arrive in the country?
- Where did they tend to settle?
- How are they viewed today?

Build a compare & contrast chart for a gallery walk.
- Compare and contrast the experience of an immigrant at the turn of the century to an immigrant who has arrived in the last few years.
- In what ways are they similar?
- In what ways are they different?

Do a gallery walk.
As a class, look at the different information you've all found. Discuss how this information affects you and your family and the way you lived or live now.

Never Enough Flamingos ♦ Never Enough Sisters ♦ Never Enough Lilacs

www.janellediller.com

Climate Impact

Explore.
Farmers in the 1930s hit a perfect storm. Decades of poor farming techniques hit a difficult climate era. Stacked on top of all of this, the economy collapsed, so even if they had been able to grow crops, prices dropped, making it difficult to sell what they'd sold before at the same price. For instance, wheat hit a high of $2.45 a bushel, but by 1932, the average national price of wheat had dropped to $.38 a bushel.

Here are some resources to explore further. Don't forget to explore Federal Writer's Project for photos and personal accounts:
http://www.livinghistoryfarm.org/farminginthe30s/money_23.html
http://science.howstuffworks.com/environmental/green-science/dust-bowl-cause.htm

Analyze.
- What were the farming techniques that contributed to the collapse of farming? How did they contribute to the problem?
- What were the climate events that contributed? What was their impact?
- What was the rainfall during this period? What was the impact on farming and farmers?
- What caused the dust bowl? How did this impact farming?
- What stopped the dust bowl? How did this impact farming?
- How is the climate changing today that is impacting farming? If nothing changes, what do you think the impact on farming will be 20 years from now?

Discuss.
- Divide into six groups. Each group should take one of the above questions and research it.
- Present your findings in a pictorial way that will engage the class. Use graphs, pie charts, and pictures from then and now. Use a tool like Piktochart to display your findings to the class.
- As a class discuss the following question: What challenges do farmers face today with climate change? What can we learn from the past to avoid some of the challenges?

The Art of Quilting

For Mennonites in the 1930s, art of any kind was an extravagance of money and time. That doesn't mean they had no art in their lives. Quilts were an appropriate way to share artistic talent. They also represented the frugalness of the era and of the sect since most quilts were nothing more than leftover fabric from a dress, shirt, or apron. There was a hierarchy, though.

Comforters
These were the most utilitarian end and so not really quilts. They might have been pieced, but instead of the intricate hand-stitched patterns, they were simply knotted to keep the various layers together.

Machine Pieced and Machine Stitched
These came next in value. While it wasn't uncommon to use a sewing machine to piece a quilt together, in the 1930s it would have been highly uncommon to use a machine to quilt the pattern that overlaid the quilt.

Machine pieced and hand quilted
This would have been more typical.

Hand pieced and hand quilted
It took real skill—and time!—to stitch the pieces together by hand and then hand quilt the pattern on top. Poorly stitch pieces meant the quilt would come apart in the laundry, so it was important to do it right.

All quilts other than comforters had a repetitive fabric pattern and a hand-stitched, or quilted, design that might follow the fabric pattern, or it might have additional elements to it. Traditionally, the back side of a quilt is plain fabric so if that is the side that shows, the elaborate pattern is visible.

Quilts were more than an art form (and any self-respecting Mennonite in the 1930s would have been appalled at quilting being referred to anything so frivolous as "art"), they were also a way of socializing. Women's sewing circles sprang up after World War I in church basements and homes. Women gathered to work on quilts to send to places around the world that needed them. It meant that the skilled and serious quilters sometimes had to look the other way as they looked at the stitching of the novice quilters.

The tradition carries on today. Mennonites in North America hold MCC Sales, which supports Mennonite Central Committee relief work around the world. The highlight of every sale is the quilt auction, where quilts go for thousands of dollars and are recognized for the art they truly are.

Never Enough Flamingos ♦ Never Enough Sisters ♦ Never Enough Lilacs

www.janellediller.com

Your Turn to Quilt

Create Your Own Quilt.

Choose your medium.
You don't have to use just fabric. You can use paint, markers, crayons, wood, glass, paper, or something else.

Choose a traditional pattern from the 1930s.
- If you choose to make a fabric quilt, start by making a single square no larger than 12" x 12", which someday could be a square in a larger quilt.
- Make sure that you have both aspects to a quilt: a repetitive color pattern and "stitching" that repeats the pattern of the fabric.

Or create your own pattern.
- Make each square an event in your life that was significant.
- Remember to use a quilt theme with a repetitive color pattern and "stitching" that repeats the pattern of the fabric.

Create.
Describe your process for creating your quilt art.
- What quilt pattern did you choose?
- Why did you choose the pattern?
- What was difficult about make it?
- What was easy?

Music in Society

Music lyrics often reflect what is happening in the larger society. Here are five popular songs from the 1930s.

1. "Happy Days Are Here Again" - Ben Selvin or Benny Meroff
2. "Puttin' on the Ritz" - Harry Richman
3. "On The Sunny Side of the Street" - Ted Lewis
4. "Get Happy" - Nat Shilkret
5. "Ten Cents A Dance" - Ruth Etting

Here are links to versions of a couple of songs:
https://www.youtube.com/watch?v=JW-0kbIcf1E
https://www.youtube.com/watch?v=_lWiLyJfs24

"Happy Days Are Here Again" was written in 1929 and first recorded the month after the 1929 Crash that kicked-off the Great Depression. In 1932, the song became Franklin Roosevelt's campaign song.

Analyze as a class.
- What do these songs tell you about the decade?
- What political or social significance did the songs have?

Woody Guthrie

Analyze.
One of the more influential musicians from the 1930s is Woody Guthrie (1912-1967). His songs have been recorded countless times by musicians in the decades following. One of the reasons his work is so memorable is because his lyrics captured the challenges and the spirit of the times.

His top songs from the 1930s are as follows. Here's a site with the actual lyrics
http://woodyguthrie.org/Lyrics/Lyrics.htm
https://www.thenation.com/article/top-ten-woody-guthrie-songs/

- "So long, It's been good to know you" https://www.youtube.com/watch?v=zqiblXFlZuk
- "Do Re Mi" https://www.youtube.com/watch?v=46mO7jx3JEw
- "I ain't got no home" https://www.youtube.com/watch?v=GTnVMulDTYA
- "Talking Dust Bowl" https://www.youtube.com/watch?v=dkAxuqrVNBM
- "This land was made for you and me" https://www.youtube.com/watch?v=wxiMrvDbq3s

What do the lyrics tell you about Guthrie's perspective of the 1930s?

Compare.
Choose five songs from popular music today that speak to our decade.

- How do they reflect the United States today?
- Fifty years from now, if this were all people had about the era, what would these songs tell people about this decade?

Create.
- If you were the Woody Guthrie of today, what kind of songs would you write?
- What topics need to be talked about? If you need help, use a newspaper or TV to help you determine hot button topics.
- Write a song of social importance about today. Set it to existing music or to your own original music.
- Record it and share with your classmates.

Never Enough Flamingos ♦ Never Enough Sisters ♦ Never Enough Lilacs

www.janellediller.com

The Never Enough Series

The following activities are created to use with the *Never Enough* trilogy. The exercise "Women's Place in Society" can be used without reference to the *Never Enough* series. However, if used as a pre-reading activity for the trilogy, it provides a helpful context for the events in the three books. In addition, the "Discovering More" exercise can be used as a stand alone activity, but it's more appropriate to use as a companion to the "*Never Enough Flamingos* Critical Reading activity."

One note: if you choose to read all three books as a class or make them available for individual students to read, it's important to read them in order since the characters and events build on each other.

2017 Kansas Notable Book
2017 CIPA Evvy Gold
2017 IPPY Bronze Award

It's the Depression and it's rural Kansas. For good measure, nature decides to throw in a Dust Bowl. It's not the life Cat Peters would have chosen, but the young Mennonite girl doesn't have much say in it.

Driven to the edge of bankruptcy by the relentless winds of the Dust Bowl, Cat's family is desperate. Fortunately, wealthy Simon Yoder generously saves them with a loan. Everyone gets something more out of the arrangement than what they bargain for. Cat's father gains a start back from the edge and the shame that he can't provide for his family. Cat's older brother goes to work for Simon to pay off the family debts and learns lots of new ideas. And Simon gets the debt repaid and casts a sticky net over the Peters family. So in the end, everyone loses.

Still the rains don't come. Without rain, there is no wheat. So Cat, too, goes to the Yoder's to clean and cook and do whatever the hired girls do. It turns out the hired girls at the Yoder house do a lot more than cook and clean, for Simon Yoder is a man who steals the souls of young girls.

And now Cat has slipped into his hands.

"It is a testament to Diller's authorial strength that, through the despair, she weaves in disarming humor . . . Peopled with some enduring characters . . . this is a vivid, surprising page-turner."
~Kirkus Reviews

Never Enough Flamingos ♦ *Never Enough Sisters* ♦ *Never Enough Lilacs*
www.janellediller.com

The Never Enough Series (con't)

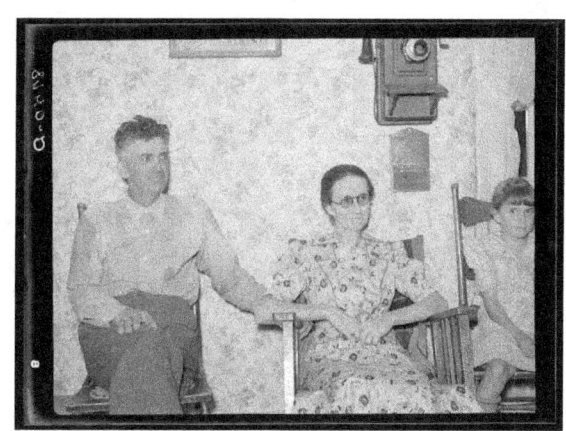

It all seemed so simple in the moment. Simon Yoder is an evil man who steals the souls of young girls. Get rid of Simon Yoder, and all will be right with the world. Except it only works that way in fairy tales, and Mennonites don't put much stock in fairy tales.

Henry Schmidt throws his daughter Suzanne out of the house because of her bad funeral behavior. She eventually lands in the home of Cat Peters, her best friend and would be savior, just in time for the long arm of the law to snatch her away.

And now Cat must save Suzanne from a life in prison—or worse.

The world unravels.

The U.S. enters the war, and families fall apart. Ben Peters disappears behind enemy lines, which sweeps the family into deep despair. Suzanne Schmidt is released from her sentence and spirals out of control as she tries to climb out of her unsettling darkness.

It's up to Cat to knit the fractured lives together again, but the task will require doing the impossible.

Narrative Viewpoints

Writers use narrative viewpoints, or perspectives, to narrate a story. In fiction, three primary viewpoints are used:

First Person Narration
With first person narration, the story is told from the perspective of one of the characters. It uses the pronouns I and me. First person narration gives readers the inner thoughts and motives of the character. The disadvantage to first person narration is that the reader doesn't know what other characters are thinking or even doing if the narrator isn't present.

While first-person narration is usually a single character throughout a story or work. It doesn't have to be. For instance, Amy Tan's *The Joy Luck Club*, has first-person narration by eight different characters. She does a masterful job creating unique recognizable voices for each person and adds to the complexity by following the characters as they age. First person narrators don't have to be human. Death is the narrator in *The Book Thief*. A dog is the narrator for *The Art of Racing in the Rain*.

The reader can tell from the very first sentence in *Never Enough Flamingos* that this is written in first-person narrative: "I come from a long line of storytellers, which isn't my fault."

Third-Person Omniscient Narration
In contrast, third-person omniscient narration tells the story without being part of it. The narrator can move from one character to another and explain the inner thoughts and motives of each one. It makes it easier to describe complex, nonlinear plots. The disadvantage is that the reader might not feel as integrated into the actual events of the story.

If *Never Enough Flamingos* were written in third-person omniscient, it might look like this. "Cat Peters comes from a long line of storytellers, which isn't her fault. Her brother, Ben, who somehow escaped the family curse . . . " In the story, the narrator could explain Ben's perspective or what Simon Yoder is thinking or what Cat's mother is feeling. The narrator could also tell us what's going on at the Simon Yoder house when Cat isn't there.

Third-Person Limited
Third-person limited narrative sits in between first person and third-person omniscient. The narrator is still all knowing, but the focus is on a single character. The advantage is that there's more intimacy because the reader identifies with a single character and the writer still has flexibility about explaining the plot to the reader. However, the disadvantage is that it's still not as intimate as first-person narrative and, because it follows a single character, it's limited in what the reader can know beyond where the character is.

Narration Viewpoints (cont'd)

Practice Narration Styles.

1. Choose a dramatic scene in the book. Use third-person omniscient and write the scene.

2. Now using the same scene, use first-person narrative to write the scene from the perspective of one of the other main characters.

3. Share your scene with a partner or in a small group and get their perspective about the contrast.

For both narration styles, you'll have to make up thoughts, feelings, and motives for the other characters since you don't know for sure what these are based on the existing text.

- How does the scene change as a result of the shift in narrative style?
- What changes for the reader?
- Which was easier to write? Why?

Your Turn

Story Starters:

Now it's your turn. Choose one of the following prompts and write a short story or chapter based on what you've learned from the plot and characters in the book. You may choose to continue with first-person narrative or change to third-person omniscient or third-person limited narrative.

1. Cat's grandfather doesn't die, and so her father makes her return to Simon Yoder's. Write about what happens in the week that follows.

2. *Never Enough Flamingos* ends with the funeral of Simon Yoder. Although the first chapter of *Never Enough Sisters* follows in the book, ignore it for the moment. Write your own short story of what happens following *Never Enough Flamingos*.

3. Cat is now twenty years older and meets her friend Suzanne. Write what happens.

4. Simon Yoder survives the fall. Write the next chapter or a new ending.

Predict the Story

Good readers like to try to predict what will happen next. Most of the time, they don't even know they're doing it. The better they get at predicting, the better they get at reading. As you read *Never Enough Flamingos,* ask yourself at the end of each chapter what you think will happen next. Why do you think this? What are the clues from what you've already read? Don't forget to revise your predictions as you read. You don't have to wait till the end of each chapter to predict the direction of the story. In fact, it might change several times in a chapter.

After you've read the book, review your predictions. Were you close?

Use this form to keep track of what you think will happen:

Chapter Page Prediction
_____
_____
_____
_____
_____
_____
_____
_____
_____
_____
_____
_____
_____
_____
_____
_____
_____
_____
_____
_____
_____
_____
_____
_____

Predict the Story (cont'd)

Chapter Page Prediction

Women's Place in Society

One of the significant changes since the 1930s is the role of women in society. Women finally received the right to vote in 1920 (nearly 250 years after the founding of the country!). Up until then, and in the early decades, they had a very small role in policy making or even value in society. It would take decades for women to truly have equal rights—and some would say it still hasn't happened.

The Depression caused a seismic shift in gender roles. One of the results of the stock market crash and the following economic crash was that unemployment for men rose to 25%. In other words, one out of every four men lost his job. This created a hostile reaction because the number of women in the workforce (approximately 25%) equaled the percent of men who were unemployed. There was a perception that women had taken the jobs of men. Up until this time, society viewed men as the breadwinners and women as homemakers. With so many men unemployed, women moved into the workforce because someone had to provide for the family, and even though this wasn't a typical role, women stepped in rather than let the family starve. Many challenges existed:

- The minimum wage for women was significantly lower than it was for men: $525 annual pay for women versus $1,027 for men. This meant that companies could hire significantly cheaper labor if they hired women.
- During the Depression, 26 states had laws that prohibited hiring married women since the thinking was that a man should be the breadwinner.
- The 1932 Federal Economy Act banned more than one family member from working for the United States government. The intent was to reduce the number of women working.
- Federal agencies such as Civilian Conservation Corps and Civil Works Administration gave jobs almost entirely to men because the perception was that women couldn't do manual labor.
- Social security benefits were designed to go to the man and his dependent wife, which meant that women only deserved economic rights in relations to men. Those who didn't fit the traditional housewife mold were significantly disadvantaged.

Be an anthropologist.
After reflecting on these points, write a one-page analysis on the following questions:
1. If the husband lost his job and the wife went to work, what impact do you think this had in marriages?
2. How did this change how men viewed themselves?
3. How did this change how women viewed themselves?
4. How did society benefit from this shift? What were the losses that people perceived?
5. Given all of this, what was the impact of the perceived value of women during this era?

CRITICAL READING

Analyze

The central storyline of *Never Enough Flamingos* is about sexual abuse. Today with the #metoo and #churchtoo movements, many resources to turn to, and the visibility of the issue, it's possible the story might be different. In the 1930s, though, Cat Peters had few options. Women were considered to be second class citizens and children had even lower status. Answer the following questions and be prepared to be part of a class discussion.

1. Sexual abusers often "groom" their victims by flattering them, giving them gifts, or making them feel valuable. How did Simon Yoder groom Cat?

2. Sexual abusers often target people who are more vulnerable because they feel unvalued or unloved. What made Cat more vulnerable?

3. What was Cat's response to Simon Yoder's behavior?

4. Sexual abusers also often subtly find ways to buy the silence of other family members or friends or influence them into believing the abuser rather than the victim. What did Simon Yoder do that influenced Cat's brother, Ben, and her father to discount what she is saying?

5. How were females viewed in the 1930s that would have contributed to this?

6. What was Cat's mother's perspective on Simon Yoder? What were the clues that made her suspicious about him?

7. What made it difficult for Cat's mother to stand up to Cat's father?

8. What was the turning point for Cat's father in his willingness to believe her?

9. Suzanne's older sisters were all abused by Simon Yoder. What was the ripple effect of that abuse for them?

10. If the story were written about today's world, what options or resources would Cat or Suzanne have to reach out to?

Never Enough Flamingos ♦ *Never Enough Sisters* ♦ *Never Enough Lilacs*

www.janellediller.com

Discovering More

To better understand the impact of sexual abuse, it's helpful to talk to someone who has experienced it. If you know a family member or friend who has experienced sexual abuse and is willing to talk about it, interview this person. The following questions are a starting point. It's very important the person feels safe in responding. Ask what the person needs to be willing to share his or her story. This may include things like being anonymous, not sharing details of events, or understanding how the information will be used. If the person isn't comfortable sharing, respect the decision.

This exercise is for you to have a clearer understanding of the impact of sexual abuse. It's not about telling someone's story in graphic detail. Your first obligation is to honor the person's privacy. Your output of this interview does not depend on sharing details.

Here are some questions to get you started.

1. What were the circumstances around the abuse? (Your age, your relationship with the abuser, your relationship with the people who should have been protecting you, the era it occurred, etc.)
2. What details are you comfortable sharing? (Be very respectful of what this person is willing to share!)
3. What did this person do to "groom" you? (It may be that the abuser didn't "groom" the person but simply took advantage of the person without any willingness or consent.)
4. How did the "grooming" impact you?
5. What, if anything, did you do or say to let others know the sexual abuse was occurring or had occurred? If you didn't let others know about the abuse, what kept you from telling?
6. What was the response of those you told? Why do you think they had this response?
7. How did you feel about yourself after the abuse?
8. How has this impacted your life?
9. If you were to face this situation now, how would you respond to the abuser?
10. What would you tell your child if he or she faced a similar situation?

Write.
Write a one-page report that includes the following:
1. What did you learn about the impact of sexual abuse?
2. What will be important for you to understand if you interact with others who have experienced sexual abuse?

RESOURCES TO TAP

The country has come a long way since the 1930s regarding sexual abuse. Since 1993, the number of sexual assaults in the U.S. has fallen by half. Unfortunately, we still have a long way to go.

Surfacing the issue in a classroom requires courage and skill. If you are unsure about how to handle the issue, a good starting point is to check with your school's guidance counselor or the health and wellness teacher to learn what the school is already doing to build awareness and offer resources where needed.

In addition, the following websites provide helpful resources to use:
- RAINN (Rape, Abuse, & Incest National Network) https://www.rainn.org
- Me too Movement https://metoomvmt.org/
- #ChurchToo http://emilyjoypoetry.com/churchtoo
- Centers for Disease Control and Prevention https://www.cdc.gov/violenceprevention/sexualviolence/prevention.html
- National Sexual Violence Resource Center https://www.nsvrc.org
- Victims of Crime https://victimsofcrime.org/media/reporting-on-child-sexual-abuse
- Military Health System https://www.health.mil/Military-Health-Topics/Conditions-and-Treatments/Mental-Health/Sexual-Assault-Prevention

Conscientious Objectors in World War II

Explore.

In 1940, as it became clearer and clearer that the United States would enter World War II, President Franklin Roosevelt signed into law the Selective Service and Training Act of 1940. This law created the first peacetime draft in our country's history, and it required every male age 18 to 65 to register. During World War II, 34.5 million men registered. Not everyone was willing to serve; however, the Act exempted only men who, "by reason of religious training or belief, is conscientiously opposed to the participation of war in any form." Men could not ask for conscientious objector (CO) status outside of religious beliefs or because of opposition to a particular war.

Over 72,300 applied for conscientious objector status, but only about half received it. Of those, 25,000 served in noncombatant roles and 12,000 chose to perform alternative service, called Civilian Public Service (CPS). It's important to note that 6,000 men were not given CO status and chose to go to prison rather than go into the military. The majority of men choosing CO status were from religious groups such as Mennonites, Church of the Brethren, Quakers, and Seventh Day Adventists.

Those who participated in CPS served in a variety of ways, often filling in for those who went into the military. They worked on conservation, forestry, and public health. Many worked as smoke jumpers and fought fires in the Pacific Northwest that were started by the thousands of timed incendiary balloons released by the Japanese. About 500 COs volunteered for medical experiments, testing, among other things, the affects of starvation and cures for typhus and malaria. Three thousand COs volunteered to work in mental hospitals and discovered first hand the appalling conditions of mental health care in the country. After the war, these men were instrumental in significantly changing how mentally ill people are treated and cared for.

Here are some resources to explore further. Don't forget to search Federal Writer's Project for photos and personal accounts:
- Brief history of conscientious objection: https://www.swarthmore.edu/Library/peace/conscientiousobjection/co%20website/pages/HistoryNew.htm
- Mennonites: http://thirdway.com/prepare-for-peace/history/conscientious-objection-2/
- Quakers: https://www.friendsjournal.org/u-s-conscientious-objectors-world-war-ii/
- Medical and starvation experiments on COs: https://medium.com/war-is-boring/america-experimented-on-conscientious-objectors-during-world-war-ii-30494131d25c
- Soldiers of conscientious http://archive.pov.org/soldiersofconscience/background/

Discovering a Different Perspective

Explore.
A great way to understand different perspectives is to have a conversation with someone who has had a different life experience and has made different choices than you. Find a conscientious objector to interview. One place to start is to contact local congregations of historic peace churches:

- **Mennonite** http://mennoniteusa.org/who-we-are/directory/
- **Quaker** https://www.fgcquaker.org/connect/quaker-finder
- **Church of the Brethren** http://www.brethren.org/church/
- **Amish**
- **Seventh Day Adventists** http://www.adventistdirectory.org/findbytype.aspx?EntityType=C

Ask for contact information for someone who would be willing to be interviewed. Living WWII-era COs are few and far between since they would be in at least their mid-90s. However, it's likely you can find COs from the Vietnam War era since these men are in their 60s, 70s, and 80s. Many would be very willing to talk about their experiences. Here are some starting questions:

- Why did you decide to become a CO?
- What was the process for getting CO status?
- How did your family respond to your choice?
- What happened in your life as a result?
- How were you treated by others in your community or by strangers because you chose to be a CO?
- How did the experience of choosing a CO status change you?
- Would you make this choice again? Why or why not?

What do you take away from the interview?
- If the draft were reinstated and all 18-year-old men and women had to serve, what choice would you make? Why?
- If the laws would change and you could choose a CO status based on your opposition to selective wars, how would this impact your choice? Why?
- What would the conversation be like with your family concerning your choice? Why?
- If the choices are similar to the historic choices for COs, what would you choose for a job or role if you would choose to be a CO?

Exploring Choices

Explore.
In one way or another wars, drafts, and military or alternative service impact nearly every family in the United States. Interview someone from your family or circle of neighbors and friends who was drafted (born before 1952). Here are some questions to get you started:
- What were your feelings when you got your draft notice?
- What choices did you make as a result? Why?
- What was the impact of that choice?
- How was your choice similar or different from your father's and grandfather's generations in your family? How did that impact your own decision?
- What was your perspective of your peers who chose to be conscientious objectors? Why?
- How might you think of them today? If you view conscientious objectors differently today, what shifted for you? What events shifted your view?
- If the draft were reinstated, what advice would you give to an 18-year old?

Summarize.
Write a one-page summary of your interview. What is most important to share? What's most interesting? What did you learn from it?

Compare and Contrast.
In triads, share your summaries.
- How are the experiences of the interviewees similar?
- How are they different?
- How were people impacted by their experiences?
- What did you learn from hearing other stories?

Never Enough Flamingos

Discuss and Write.
Use the following questions as topics for student essays or for class or panel discussions.

1. The book begins with this statement: How you get to where you don't know you're going determines where you end up. How have you gotten to where you are? Given how you've gotten to this point, where will you most likely end up?

2. What role does humor play in the story?

3. What is the effect of the author's use of first person narrative? What's the impact on how it engages you as a reader?

4. Secrets are a major theme of the book. Which secrets caused more problems because there were kept? Reflect on your own secrets. Why do you keep them or share them? What's the impact on your life?

5. How does the story parallel events in Europe during the same period in history?

6. Several times throughout the book, characters question what the truth is. Chapter 5: "Life was simpler in those days. If Dad said something, it was the truth, whether it was true or not." Chapter 10: "Most people really don't want to know the truth if they think it'll change what they want to believe." Chapter 17: "There's really no such thing as truth in the world. People believe what they want to believe, and that becomes the truth." Do you agree or disagree with the statements? Why?

7. At the macro level, countries sacrificed an enormous amount to fight Hitler. Cat gives the example of the rescue at Dunkirk, where a heroic flotilla of small boats crossed the English Channel and saved three hundred forty thousand British troops that were almost trapped behind German lines. What are we called to sacrifice—in war or at the societal level? What are you willing to sacrifice?

8. Suzanne took action because she believed she had no other choices. If we think of morality on a scale of one to ten, with ten being completely right morally and one being completely wrong morally, where is Suzanne on that scale in the final chapters? Why?

Never Enough Flamingos (con't)

9. A familiar idiom in America is that the end justifies the means. Do you agree with this? If it's situational for you, what are the situations where you would agree with this? Where do you disagree? Is this idiom truer for you on a macro (or country) level or micro (or personal) level? Why?

10. How would various characters answer the previous question? Ezra? Ben? Cat? Simon? Suzanne? Henry? Dess? Rose?

11. On a macro (or country) level, many people would say that going to war is morally right even though on a personal level, they would never intentionally hurt someone. Is your value system the same at the macro level as it is at the micro level? If not, where are there differences? Why are there differences?

Never Enough Sisters

Discuss and Write

Use the following questions as topics for student essays or for class or panel discussions.

1. What are the parallels between the story and events in Europe during the same period in history?

2. This trilogy is about Mennonites. In what ways does their theology resonate with you? In what ways is it uncomfortable for you?

3. In Chapter 2, Cat observes this: "We lived in a time when Mennonites believed in hierarchy. This was the order of our universe: God, man, woman, farm animals, mammals, avian, fish, reptiles, insects, spiders, and amoebas. Consequently, except for the more forward-thinking among us, just as the worst human was considered to be of a higher order than the best farm animal, the worst and dumbest man was considered better and smarter than the best and smartest woman. This thinking occasionally led us down some bad paths." What's your hierarchy? Where does it take you? What's the hierarchy of the family structure you were raised in? What has been the impact of that?

4. In Chapter 5, Cat defends her Dad's decision not to let Ben play basketball for Kansas State University. She explains that he was protecting his son from what he personally didn't understand. What decisions for others or for yourself have you made that were because you didn't understand something and so assumed it was wrong or risky? What was the impact of making that particular decision?

5. In Chapter 10, Norma Miller says this about what has been going on at Simon Yoder's: "I guess the truth is, we didn't want to know. . . . If you knew, then you had to do something, and what could we have done?" Where do you see this thinking or behavior in yourself, your family, community, country, or the world? What's gained and what's lost by living this way?

6. 6. As with *Never Enough Flamingos*, secrets are a major theme of the book. In Chapter 12, Sam James tells Cat, "It's not always good to keep a secret, especially one you never wanted in the first place." Reflect on your own secrets. Are there secrets you keep that you never wanted in the first place? Why do you keep them? What's the impact on your life? What would happen if you shared the secrets?

Never Enough Sisters (con't)

7. In Chapter 23, Cat wonders, "If it was okay for the world to resolve problems by killing, it must be okay for individuals to do the same. Did this mean that if it was okay for Suzanne to kill Simon, then it was okay for the Americans to start killing Japanese and Germans?" Should there be different moral codes at the macro level (state/country/world) than we have for the micro level (individual)? Why or why not? What if they would be the same?

8. How have your values or perspective shifted, challenged, or been clarified as a result of reading *Never Enough Sisters*?

Never Enough Lilacs

Discuss and Write

Use the following questions as topics for student essays or for class or panel discussions.

1. The original title for this trilogy was The Secret War. What are the important secrets that shaped the lives of the characters? At various times throughout the three books, Cat muses that some secrets are better not known. What are some of the secrets that would have been better not to know? Why? What are some of the secrets that seemed better not to know but turned out to be important ones to know?

2. In Chapter 9, Cat notes, "Patriotism is a religion." How is patriotism like a religion? How is it different? What is the impact when patriotism becomes a religion?

3. In his letter to the Peters family about Ben, Ernie Kowalski writes, "[Ben] confided in me that he made a conscious decision at some point to fight this evil, even if he lost part of his own soul doing it." In Chapter 13 Cat says, "[T]here weren't any more girls after Suzanne. She was the final one. How many girls had she saved by sacrificing herself?" Both Ben and Susanne sacrificed themselves to stop evil. Yet only one is revered for this sacrifice. Why?

4. Forgiveness is an important theme in *Never Enough Lilacs*. In Chapter 23, Cat tells Ethel, "Those girls do need to forgive Simon and forgive you. But what are they forgiving if there's been no change in you? How can it be from the heart? How can those words be anything but empty?" Can there be forgiveness if there's been no change in the other person? Whom do you need to forgive? What will it take for you to forgive that person? Who needs to forgive you? What will it take that person to forgive you? What can happen if there is forgiveness?

5. In Chapter 30, Cat observes she doesn't know how entire countries forgive each other. Is it possible to forgive an entire country for their war aggressions? What happens if countries don't? What happens when countries do?

6. In the last chapter, Cat observes, "On August 14, 1945, the war ended. At least the bombs and the shooting part. Fifty-five million people died in World War II. Hundreds and hundreds of millions more suffered from wounds to their bodies or souls. It seems there should have been a better way to solve the problem of Hitler, but this was the only solution the world came up with. Unfortunately, we were sorely lacking in imagination those years." It could be argued that the world is still lacking in imagination in how to resolve problems peacefully. What are specific things we could be doing as a country or as individuals to resolve problems more peacefully?

Never Enough Lilacs (con't)

7. *Never Enough Flamingos* begins with this: "How you get to where you don't know you're going determines where you end up." Where will Cat, Suzanne, and Ben end up?

8. After having read the full trilogy, *Never Enough Flamingos, Never Enough Sisters*, and *Never Enough Lilacs*, what impact has the story had on you? Has your thinking shifted about anything? If so, in what way(s)? How has this impact changed your behaviors?

9. What will stay with you from the story?

www.ingramcontent.com/pod-product-compliance
Lightning Source LLC
Chambersburg PA
CBHW081758100526
44592CB00015B/2483